I'M A HERO

Neto Meeks

Copyright © 2024 by Neto Maceo Meeks. All rights reserved.

No part of this publication may be reproduced, stored or transmitted in any form or by any means, electronic, mechanical, photocopying, recording, scanning, or otherwise without written permission from the publisher. It is illegal to copy this book, post it to a website, or distribute it by any other means without permission. For permission requests, write to the publisher at the address below.

Brer Anancy Press
3701 Santa Rosalia Dr.
Los Angeles, CA 90008

info@breranancypress.com
www.breranancypress.com

ISBN: 978 976 8266 23 1

First published 2024
Printed in the United States of America

PUBLISHER'S STATEMENT

This anthology represents a portion of a much larger body of work created over twenty-five years. Many of the poems were recorded on video and in performances at festivals such as The Calabash Literary Festival, FiWiSinting, and Ananse SoundSplash.

In 2023, two of the featured poems in this anthology received awards in the *Jamaica Creative Writing Competition* and the Exhibition of the *Jamaica Cultural Development Commission*. *Field Marshall In The Battle won* silver, and *Cruising Up The Waltham won* bronze.

The drawings were done during the period when Neto was learning to use his left hand while undergoing rehabilitative work on his right hand.

CONTENTS

Heart-O-Love ix
About Neto Meeks xi
Foreword xv

PART ONE
ROOTED AND GROUNDED

I Want My Continent 1
Always Love You 2
That's How It Goes 4
Deserters Night Lurkers 9
Heights of Perfection 11
Back to Molynes 12

PART TWO
THE PAIN IN PARADISE

Who's To Pay/The Pain In Paradise 21
Everyone's Tears/King of Sorrow 25
Cruising Up The Waltham 30
Conspiracy 32

PART THREE
HERO

Be Brave 37

I'm A Hero 39

Dragon Fly 42

Field Marshall 44

Grow What You Eat! 45

Island, I Land 48

Warriors 50

HEART–O–LOVE

This book is for my children.

I am grateful to my son Zen-I for his constant love and support and for his assistance in transcribing the poems. I salute my daughter Nialli whose courage and determination are inspirational.

These poems mark significant events and important people in my life. They include my relationship with my grandmother Pearl and the adventures in and around her house in the Molynes Road area since I was only two weeks old until the present time; the Royal Afrikan Souljahs, a dub poetry collective which I helped to establish in the late 1990's with my brethren Ras Takura and the Mighty Ginsu and with which I continue to perform.

I give thanks to my parents for the way I understand the world, my aunts, uncles and cousins who have taught me that truly, family is everything. And to all the friends who are always there. Special thanks to Sage and the blessed memory of my martial arts teacher, Kunda. Honor. Respex. Royal. Afrikan. Souljahs.

Published in the year of the 60th anniversary of the repatriation of the remains of Jamaica's first National Hero, The Rt. Excellent Marcus Mosiah Garvey. Honour de man still.

Neto Maceo Meeks

ABOUT NETO MEEKS

It is such an honour to introduce Neto Meeks to those who have not yet met him.

Those who have, will know him as multi-talented media practitioner, writer, performance poet, social development worker, sketch artist, martial arts enthusiast and model who has also operated his own farm producing food for family and friends. Some may also know that he has employed music, poetry and yoga as central components of his recovery from a major stroke. That he continues to write and perform offers a unique perspective for raising awareness of the power of the arts for personal and national development. It is also a manifestation of Neto's own determination to live life to its fullest and has been an important aspect of his being over the many years that I have been associated with him.

When he was about 12 years old, I taught Neto Meeks second form English Language at St. Joseph's Academy, a Catholic private secondary school for boys in St. John's, Antigua. I was also his homeroom teacher so I got to spend a significant amount of time observing his development.

Neto was a very quiet student who appeared at times to live in his own world. I could see from very early that his thinking was outside the box, something which was not particularly welcomed at a Catholic school in a small Caribbean island. Neto's exercise books, for example, not only contained his work but also his drawings, which appeared to be products of his daydreams. You could see how this could be troubling to a young teacher who had not been prepared to teach students, but rather subjects.

I set to work at attempting to keep Neto organised, sometimes engaging in strong remonstrations because I saw his great potential and wanted to see him "conform." Even then, he clearly had his views that there were certain issues that demanded confronting rather than conformity. I can only imagine how he must have felt uncomfortable because I was always on his case. Truth be told, I saw a highly intelligent, creative and self-assured young man who was well-liked and accepted by his classmates.

On a visit to the school, I reassured Neto's mother that the pressure I was putting on her son was motivated solely by my desire to see the fulfillment of his great potential. She had her own ideas about encouraging his potential for concern about the condition and future of the collective. After that visit, however, my remonstrations appeared to be taken in a positive light and Neto became more organised, which manifested in better performance in his classwork and homework assignments. That's all I required from this brilliant young man.

Fast forward to the 21st century when Facebook reconnected us in the mid-to-late 2000s. I was thrilled to see how successful Neto has become on various levels. He displays a strong sense of community and continues to enjoy the loving support of his parents and friends. He is one of Jamaica's recognised and innovative dub poets celebrated by a plethora of fans (present company included). His many and varied poems have given voice to the issues that matter to much of humanity. He is living authentically on his own terms, surrounded by a beautiful world of art and music. He is a loving father whose son accompanies him in many of his performances.

It is my pleasure to see how he has grown from strength to strength. I salute this bold move to commit to the written form his performed poems which represent a gift for all who will read the collection.

Deborah Avril Lockhart, LHD
Managing Director, The Language Shop

FOREWORD

Shango brought thunder with every breath. His virile words became flesh, awakening an army of Royal African Soldiers. The audacious dreams of Martin Luther King, the impatient militancy of Malcolm X, the uniting presence of Mandela and the Griot Godhood of Bob Marley. This Pantheon of Royal African Soldiers sowed seeds that echoed offsprings like Tupac Shakur, NWA (Niggaz Wit Attitude) and The Black Lives Matter movement.

Such was the dynamic collision of the signature syntax of Neto Meeks's poems. First-Born of Revolutionary Poet Professor Brian Meeks and Indigenous Griot Warrior Queen Dr. Amina Blackwood Meeks. This Rasta Rapper Revolutionary Royal African offspring was destined for important responsibilities. As is the often twists in epic hero's journeys, his meteoric rise in the Jamaican performance arts community had intermittent interruptions.

But as we gather to ingest this long overdue collection of Poems from Neto Meeks, it is clear that despite his colossal life battles, this Royal African Soldier has not lost his immense literary courage. A couple decades ago the Poetry Society of Jamaica hosted a night called "THE MEEKS SHALL INHERIT THE EARTH" featuring Neto Meeks and his father Brian Meeks. His father commented on the rapid-fire delivery of Neto's presentation, and being a Visual-Arts apostle, my mind flew off with Images of the iconic photo of Malcolm X armed with his M1-Carbine rifle as he peers through a window and Malcolm transforms into Neto unleashing his signature rap-like rapid paced poems.

This poetry collection Neto has gifted to us, "I'M A HERO" is a testament to his unwavering courage. A homage to the notion that all real poets should be feared. "Tread" cautiously through these "Soldier-Poems" and beware of explosive literary revelations.

Tommy Ricketts,
President, Poetry Society of Jamaica

PART ONE

Rooted and Grounded

I Want My Continent

Low life, Po-lice, with No Life,
So they want to take mine
Cause its Haile,
and dem can't touch me stylie,
So wicked and wiley,
My name not Andrew Blood
But I'm feeling So IRIE,
Still the Judge want try me,
Not a pyrotechnic but I keep it so fiery,
Not Scarface but I'll write it in my diary,
I'm not a Big King Pin more slim and wirey;
Sorta like Mark Myrie,
Man a real Binghi-Man
Dat mean dem can't tire me,
Man a real Fire Men,
Dem can't expire Me,
Nuff boy vex just through Dem Girl Desire Me,
Babylon Empire can't fire me
Cause dem never hire me,
Dat mean dem can't wire me,
Or gimme dutty paper fi speak so liardly,
Rawyal Afriikan SoulJAH,
No island, I want my continent entirely,
So obvious that Mr. Marcus inspire Me

Always Love You

Looking through the mist
Ignorance is Bliss,
Cupid aimed at my heart
But it seems he missed,
So I got dissed by this Miss
And the inner got twist between my ribs and flesh,
Now it feels like I'll be with this love to my death,
I pray I have many more days left,
To live, to love, to laugh,
To heal the pain, the remains from my past,
It's an open book but look
I try to protect my heart at all costs,
Cause it's what pumps My Life, Some trife,
Not Nice, trying to hump my wife,
Turn my warm heart into ice,
Colder than a Polar Bear,
I'm A Soldier, I told her as I hold Her near,
And my love is like a Gift
That I'm gonna share with you only
It's real not phony,
Thank you for, the tenderness that you showed me
When I was so lonely
With no one out there to stand up for me,
You're closer than a bredren or as the Yankee say, Homie,

Make me think bout when Bobbie Brown wrote Tenderoni,
Before Whitney when I was just a Pickni,
That's a whole different story
Stick with me as I switch it up quickly,
Life hard back a yard but I'll be your Body Guard, and stay true,
Cause till Judgement Day I will always you Love you.

That's How It Goes

Haile Selassie I and Empress Menen
That's how it was from the beginning
Heart to heart
Should never be apart
First, she say I'm going too fast
Ah can't go too slow
Anything it is
You know I got to get my dough
That's how it is
That's just how it go
That's how it is
That's just how it go
I love you so much
And I just had to let you know
A jus so me live
More time I'm on the go
I need us to live big
I know I have to get my dough
That's how it is
That's just how it go
That's how it is
That's just how it go
I love you so much
And I just had to let you know

A jus so me live

More time I'm on the go

I need us to live big

 I had to get my dough

I know I came home

So l came home late last evening

Now so early in the morning

And I am leaving

Don't get mad

 Just try to know the reasoning

The pot need food

And plus the food need seasoning

I love you so much

And I just had to let you know

Just a part of life

You're the heart

Of my life

From this day forth

We could start a life

Nothing can part a wife

From her huzzy

If you really love you

Try yu best not to pre-judge me

You're so lovely, so bubbly

Like champagne

But

It just can't be contained in a bottle

No complain

No chain

No shackle

Like high octane
Full throttle is my pace
Words of Neto Meeks
Don't waste
Cause a need you by my side
Cause your love can't be replaced
For me to hide how I feel
Would be a disgrace
I got no time to waste
So I hold you by your waist
Pull close then say it to your face
That's how it is
That's how it go
I love you so much
And I just had to let you know
A jus so me live
More time I'm on the go
I need us to live big
So I got to get my dough
I love you so much
And I just had to let you know
A jus so me live
More time I'm on the go
I'm on the go
It's a misty morning
I'm missing my darling
I'm missing the calling
Instead of being in my arms
Looking through the mist
Ignorance is bliss

Cupid aimed at my heart
Stupid, seem that he missed
When the arrow got twist
Between my ribs and my flesh
Now It seems that
I'll feel this love
Till the days of my death
I pray I have many days left
To live to love to laugh
Heal all the pain that remain from the past
Even as an outcast
Even from multicast

It's an open book
But look I try to protect my heart at all cost
Cause, It's what pumps my life
Some trife
Not nice
Try to pump my wife
Turn my warm heart to ice
Colder than a polar bear
I'm a Souljah
That's what I told her
When I hold her near
And my love is a gift
I'm gonna share with you only
See
That's how it is
That's how it go
I love you so much

And I just had to let you know
More time I'm on the go
I need us to live big
So I have to get my dough
That's how it is
That's how it go
I love you so much
And I just had to let you know
More time I'm on the go
I'm on the go
Cause I'm a pro
My love is what I'm gonna share with you only
Yu closer than my bredren
The Yankee would say Homie
Never leave me lonely
When there was no one there to even stand up for me
Late at night when you would call me
And I remember
From September right to December
You see
That's how it is
That's how it go
I love you so much
And I just had to let you know
More time I'm on the go
Ah jus so it go
I'm on the go.

Deserters Night Lurkers

Deserters, Night Lurkers, Obeah workers,
Tear-jerkers, acid squirters,
They can't hurt us,
Can't throw me off my track
Or distract me from my purpose,
I'm still around,
Won't be no clown up in your circus,
I'm that Miracle Man
That escaped from the hands of Big Bertha,
So now everyday I'm on the Grind,
I got no Time for Murder,
Create a new picture
 With paint brighter than Berger,
Wiser, visualiza,
Now I'm A Riser and a Rider,
With something to live for and something to die for,
Only the realest stars and the trusts up I keep in my cipher,
So Big Up my High School Prom Date Ern-Marie Piper,
She still look good that's why I had to type her on the FACEBOOK and say
That was a great look,
Real sexy girl but she never was a great cook,

She'll be in my autobiography and it'll be a Great Book,
Like Malcolm X by Alex Haley,
 Give Thanks fi life,
JAH RASTAFARI, never fail me,
So I praise H.I.M., Daily ...really.

Heights of Perfection

Jones Town to Browns Town,
Haile Selassie wear the Crown,
Mobay to Negril,
We a build, nah chill,
Time don't stand still.
These words were Given to I by JAH RASTAFARI, who we glorify,
As I look at the road before I,
Will they hate or adore I?
No doubt the people love it,
For sure
Why, it's the question,
Try to make a suggestion,
But only Haile I, reach the highest heights of perfection…

Back to Molynes

Back to Molynes thinking those good times
Kick back smoke dope watching cars roll by
British link up straight back to sunrise
Benz an Bimmers they excite the whole a de young youth eyes
See myself behind the wheel
Holding on to the seat
Just my trade
I doing my best to keep it real
No CD's on the street
to make the kids scream
Late coming from skateland
Thinking bout my dream
Speaking to my two-man team
Said if I get one chance you know
That's all we need
Kick this door in
Start flying
and we never stop soaring
Tell me can you hear
These lions as they roaring
Then it's back to the lane and it's the domino game
Who's that and who's not and who's cool and who's lame
Coke smoke mix up nuff a de youths dem brain
For me no possibility

I seen them broke those chains
If you look and you search then you will find it
Back to Molynes
I think I might need help
You might know where to find me
Back to Molynes

Back to Molynes
Where thugs cock nines pap nines
and buss slugs and take lives
Dangerous bus rides
Yu see me shoes youth
Try nuh badda stuff mine
Tuff talking tuff times
Kean defen de talk
Shut yu mout until such time
As you can, I never ran
Since I was a prince
Now living like a pauper
Flip the faucet
let the funds flow like water
Future of my daughter
The author of the furious freestyle rhymes
combines with the family
As he goes
Back to Molynes
Where the females supply
Got to fool around
Year to year
Is still open season pon

Vampire
De grades that we buy
On de block hit the highest of the high
Rasta youths waiting on the I

If you look and you search and you will find it
Back to Molynes
If you hurt and need help
Then you know where to find me
Back to Molynes
If you look and you search
Then you will find it
Back to Molynes
Artical if yu need help
Then you know where to find me

Back to Molynes Road
As a youth a didn't know the way to go
In time I grow like the mango trees
That I see in the park
Moreton Park
Cassia Park
Waltham Park
Trust no shadow after dark
Tings haffe start when de sunset
To start a riot or a fire
All you need is one tec
Some wars going on far too long
And still nuh dun yet
Check it out through the stats

Add it up do the maths
Afro braids or plaits
Too many niggers drop
Man a eat man food like snacks
Come to find
The crime is all black on black
Poor people living in shacks, shacks
While some crooked cops a buss shots, shots
And some big cats hitch and scratch scratch
I learnt the game
Overtime
See what a young mind became
All the same
Why yu try to dirty up my name
Go inside
For every side
Get wet when it rains

Back pon Molynes
Well ah wonders and signs
In these times
Listen
If you look and yu search
Then you will find it
Back to Molynes
If yu hurt and need help
Then you know where to find me
Back to Molynes
If yu look and yu search
Then you will find it

Yea man Molynes Road
Yu know de code
Rewind or reload
Royal Afrikan Souljahs
Watch de saga unfold

PART TWO

The Pain in Paradise

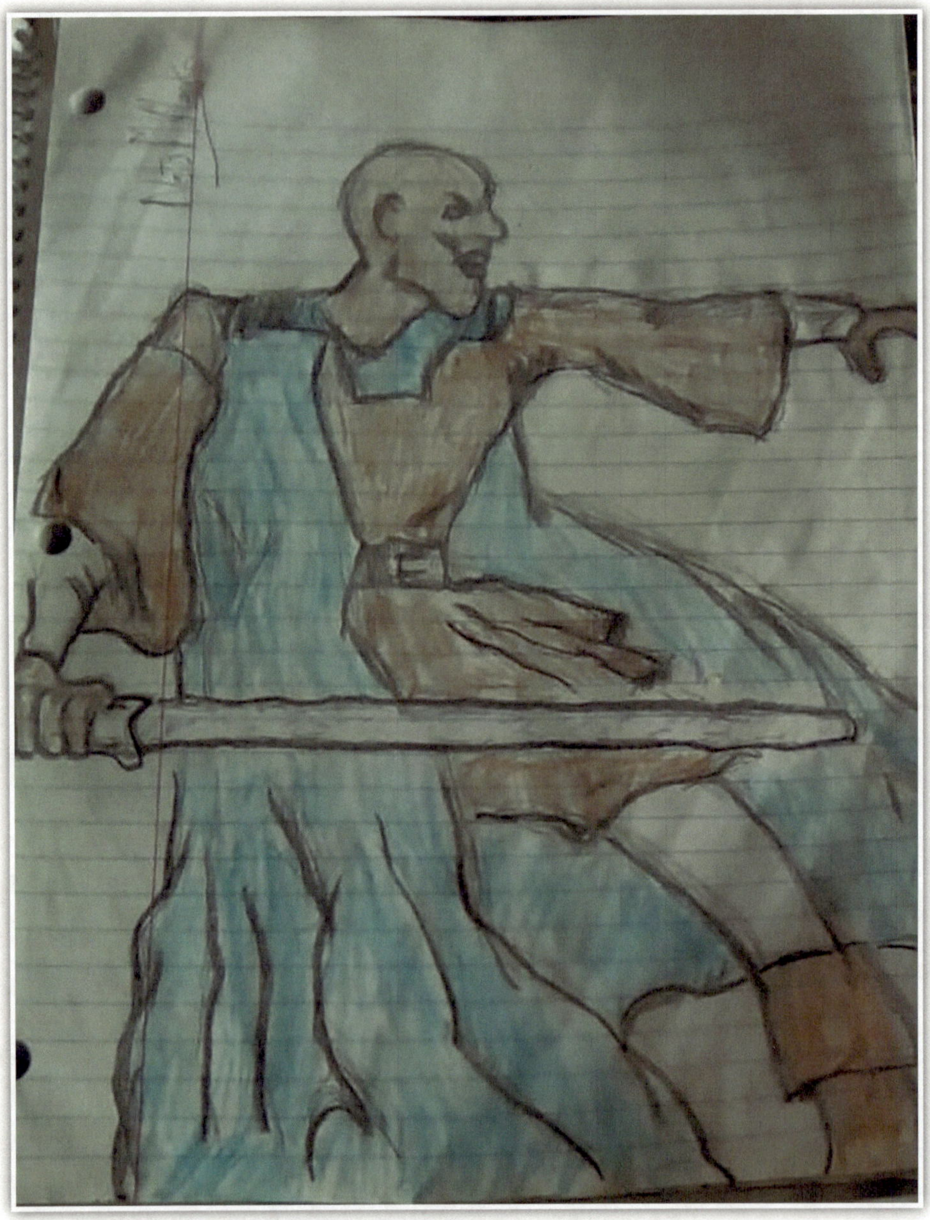

Who's To Pay/The Pain In Paradise

Yeah deep within the mind is like going deep within the ocean
coasting on that rough sea My thoughts float lonely still
Arise the question as I look into her eyes
Comes back around the power of word sound
Power of the revolution that we're aiming for shooting
Who's to pay for the poverty in paradise?
Probably the poor pressured by the parasites
Peep the percentage to get to the point
Who possess the power not the people who point
Fingers at politician preferring methods of self denial
Punks package punch drunk tales for pay
I see my people packed inna de pen
without proper trial
Who's to pay who's to pay who's to pay
Mere peer pressure don't prepare the mind
With proper answers
Pick the people in my posse
Who possess
The pride of present day panthers
Hunting for prey palitic and parlay
Party and bullshit the order of the day
Who's to pay who's to pay who's to pay

I feel the pain in partners locked away
So I pray the Most High teck pity
Poetic prophesy I preach almost perfect
So yu pick me
Eventually
Like premium wine, the powers you'd like
Scotch bonnet pick-a-pepper powerful, hot
'Pad and pencil penetrate
Speak my message to police
Protect the streets, please
Remember, no justice, no peace.

So
No planting pistols on persons
or putting coke in purses of the poor
Or it's more war, more bodies, more hearses
People like Peter no pussy
dem panic whenever paraphernalia planted
Remember, you also pay rent
And can fall to the pavement
As payment, judgement
Skull buss like Panhead
Man and man feget Black on Black
That's the plan
Of the ten percent of the people
Who run dis planet
'Pad and pencil penetrate
Preach my message to police
Protect the streets please
Remember, no justice, no peace

Seasons change but it seem sey de people dem naw change up
Come in like sey young and black
Say equals armed and dangerous
In certain constituency
Whey yu kean separate the criminals from the constabulary
Even without my spectacles
I see it clearly
So
Police and teef in de street
Mean civilians caught without teet
Can still get dem food eat
as for me, my respect inna de street
It grill up wid concrete
Because I respect de street but de day de street disrespect me
Den I piss on dat street'
Das as real as I can keep it
No justice, no peace
What yu give yu get
Das no secret
'Pad, pencil, penetrate
Take my message to the street
Protect yuself please
Remember, No justice, no peace
Me know sey yu seet

De poverty in paradise
Not nice
Being killed for our golden ice
Yow! think twice
Dem sell out Marcus Garvey fe rice and peas

Now we falling on our knees

Begging please from the enemies

Frozen at thirty-two degrees

Below zero

What the fuck

No one being the hero

But do we need them

My family bleeding

Took the heathen

Yet we're

Trying to rise

and build back Eden

The Garden of Itiopia

Babylon spoken yah

Through the scopes and they want to provoke

Us to get smoked out

But we need to just stay wise

Look into my eyes

Be wise

Above their disguise

Never gonna fall a victim to the flies

And ants e on the plans

So we come to live

And tink positive

An de message dat we give is

Naturally

About the way dat we rising

Babylon ship capsizing

We still a rise

Yow!

Everyone's Tears/ King of Sorrow

Feeling like a feather in the storm
Still I'm weathering the storm
Better than de norm
Some a wonder what a gwaan
One time I was feeling is just me and my girl
Lately I've been feeling like it's just me against the world
I couldn't trust my own lady
Whose sister tried to slay me after I was just finished sitting my baby
Sound crazy
To make up shit like this you couldn't pay me
I wanted to be like Malcolm X or Marcus Garvey
Not Slim Shady
I'm not fighting against my sisters only fighting against slavery
Now only Jah can judge me only Jah can save me

Sometimes I feel like the king of sorrow
Wondering will I live to see tomorrow
In the blood
So much horror inside I feel hollow
Like my blood had no veins and my bones no marrow
I should have read it in the tarot card
Oh my Lord

Didn't I always try to follow God
Praying in the morning, praying in the evening
For your blessing to be receiving
Knowing I believing
In my heart, my soul and all my mind
Seeking in the valley of decision
What did I find
So easy to be sent away for a crime
To do time my people who's lying
I guess that's why they say justice is blind
And there's so many innocents dying

In deathrow frying
Nevertheless I do my best and just keep trying
I can't forget Tupac
Yow! big up Jah Cure
I know some apples got worms and are rotten at the core
So next time don't open up the bolts if you're not sure
It just might be the devil knocking at your door
I wonder what's the meaning or is it just a season
Some people day-dreaming of my death and don't even know the reason
Like traitors and backstabbers who should be charged for treason
But dem sell out Marcus Garvey for rice and peas
An a likkle seasoning as we was reasoning
So we're not the first and wouldn't be the last the agents attempt to assassinate
and blast for trying to uplift the mass
Then skip it and flip it into what game of class
It happened in the past

Dem sell out Marcus Garvey for rice and peas
Dem kill Paul Bogle him wudden bow pon him knees
So know the way you're going all in times like these
Rome a try for kill out all Jah cures for disease
Dem sell out Marcus Garvey for rice and peas
Dem kill Paul Bogle him wudden bow pon him knees
So know the way you're going in times like these
Don't judge by the cover
Try and read the book please

I was raised as a disciplined child
No, I never know life wudda get so wild
Neto is meek but not all the time you can be mild
Yu seet
Give some a dem a inch and dem wi waan tek a mile
Some a wuk fe FBI a try fe put yu pan file
Someone pull a knife
It's likely dat dem will tek yu life
Got friends that died
A nuh nutten nice
Someone pull a knife
On me not once but thrice
Dem try fe cut off me tail like de tree bline mice
Now I know life is a gamble and a roll of the dice
But I'm not trying to get crucified like Jesas Crise
Afta me nuh mad
Choo me a man me fe jus tek knife stab
Afta me a nuh mouse fe experiment pan inna lab
Some a work fe Satan
everyday dem deh pan de job

I'M A HERO 27

But I and I a work fe de Most High
Jah!
Rastafari protect I from de cats and de rats
and de snakes, de dogs de scorpions de centipedes an de hogs
An even de beast wid de blade inside har bag
Whey dem waan slice we up an stab
Go back to har friends an brag
Had to move like Popeye
Fighting the Sea Hag
To make sure I never die and leave my son sad
wid no Dad
See dem sell out Marcus Garvey fe rice an peas
Dem kill Paul Bogle him wudden bow pon him knees
De way it going in times like dese
Rome a try fe kill out all jah cure fe disease
Dem sell Marcus Garvey for rice and peas
Dem kill Paul Bogle in wudden bow pon him knees
It going in all times like dese
Don't judge by the cover try and read de book please
I leff from me farm in de country come to town
I never know I was surround
by demons who want me to drown but me sey
Satan go down
Yu kean stop de Souljah's sound
Although wickedness abound
wisdom is so profound
Sister gets sister
To put Brother gains brother
Now they're using us just to destroy each other
I look into ages of the past an discover

With an anchor why they try to pull us down in the gutter
My plans over only to train and
Fight against the modern day KluKluxKlan
Make millions for my family
So we could walk free upon the African sands
Not sitting in a cell cuffed
With blood on my hands
Crying eveyone's tears
My African family
My enemies and my peers
But I never attack no one first
On that one I swear
Although dem sey don't
You know I care
Dem sell out Marcus Garvey for rice and peas
Dem kill Paul Bogle him wudden bow pon him knees

De way it going in times like dese
Rome a try fe kill out all jah cure fe disease

Den sell out Marcus Garvey for rice and peas
Dem kill Paul Bogle in wudden bow pon him knees

Know where you going in times like dese
Rome a try fe kill out all jah cure fe disease
Know where yu going in times like dese

This is the testament of I Neto Meeks

Cruising Up The Waltham

Cruising up the Waltham
So hard to overstand,
What's the Plan?
And who's the man?
And who shot ya?
Damn!
So hard to forget, can't correct the past,
Knowing that time waits for No Man,
And it flies so fast,
 Briefly, believe me.
Ash to ash, dust to dust,
Cemeteries never full,
More time it seems as if the graveyard waits for us.
How could one escape the fate of a life lived wrong?
Could I refuse to kill and still stay strong?
Could I meditate, keep my mind state,
 Without hit from the chalice and bong?
Will I remember you in the years after you're gone?
Or will I be the trigga nigga, when it's time to put it on?
 Easy Like Sunday morn but too many mourn,
 Living life insane like children of the Corn,
Every day a Man die every day a youth is born,
The cycle of life it goes, on and on and on and on,
The Most High swore, that His words would never pass,

Like Heaven and Earth,
So I look at my Child since the day of her birth,
And realize in her eyes what life worth,
And dash whey certain tings that we was told first.
Like we were born in sin,
Being Black is a curse.
I picture your coffin in the back of a hearse,
knowing you was a cat whey never powder, pet nor nurse,
O.G. vet, who posed a deadly threat,
 So they gave you five shots to the neck and chest.
Now who's to protect your woman?
Your child?
As your body disappear up the Styx, way past the Nile,
And as I shed my tears I can't suppress my smile,
Should I laugh or cry?
Live or Die?
Heaven or hell who can tell?
Same place, or different venue,
Aluta continua.
The struggle, the struggle continues,
The struggle continues.
We must Conquer. No Doubt.

Conspiracy

400 hundred years of sweat and tears
Blood spill, woman and children kill
Thrown overseas into the seas
Despair disease, **dis-ease**
Picture frame flashback freeze
Scientific research say that the black man equals ape
They say, that's why his woman can be legally raped
By the so-called higher man
So now they Nyah man
Chant
Make way for the king of kings
Ethiopia shall stretch forth her hands and spread her wings
Read it in Revelation
Now that it is for your Salvation
Still, children attempt to change their skin colour like chameleons.
Why no remembrance of Mosiah the fire,
A prophet to some, a hero to many…
To most a 50 cent coin
From Abner Louima to Rodney King,
Haiti to LA.
The black man still get ina the groin
So now we say: No justice, No peace,
This millennium youths face the east,
And sing

Hail the Black Christ King.

Yet still, not even the Rastaman could ovastand the fullness of the plan.

If not for the little man from St Anns Bay

So again I say,

Do you remember the words of Mighty Marcus

Who told us,

Up you mighty race, you can accomplish what you will.

It takes nuff mental power, whole heap a physical skill.

Never feget, honour the man still

Honour the man still

Honour the man still

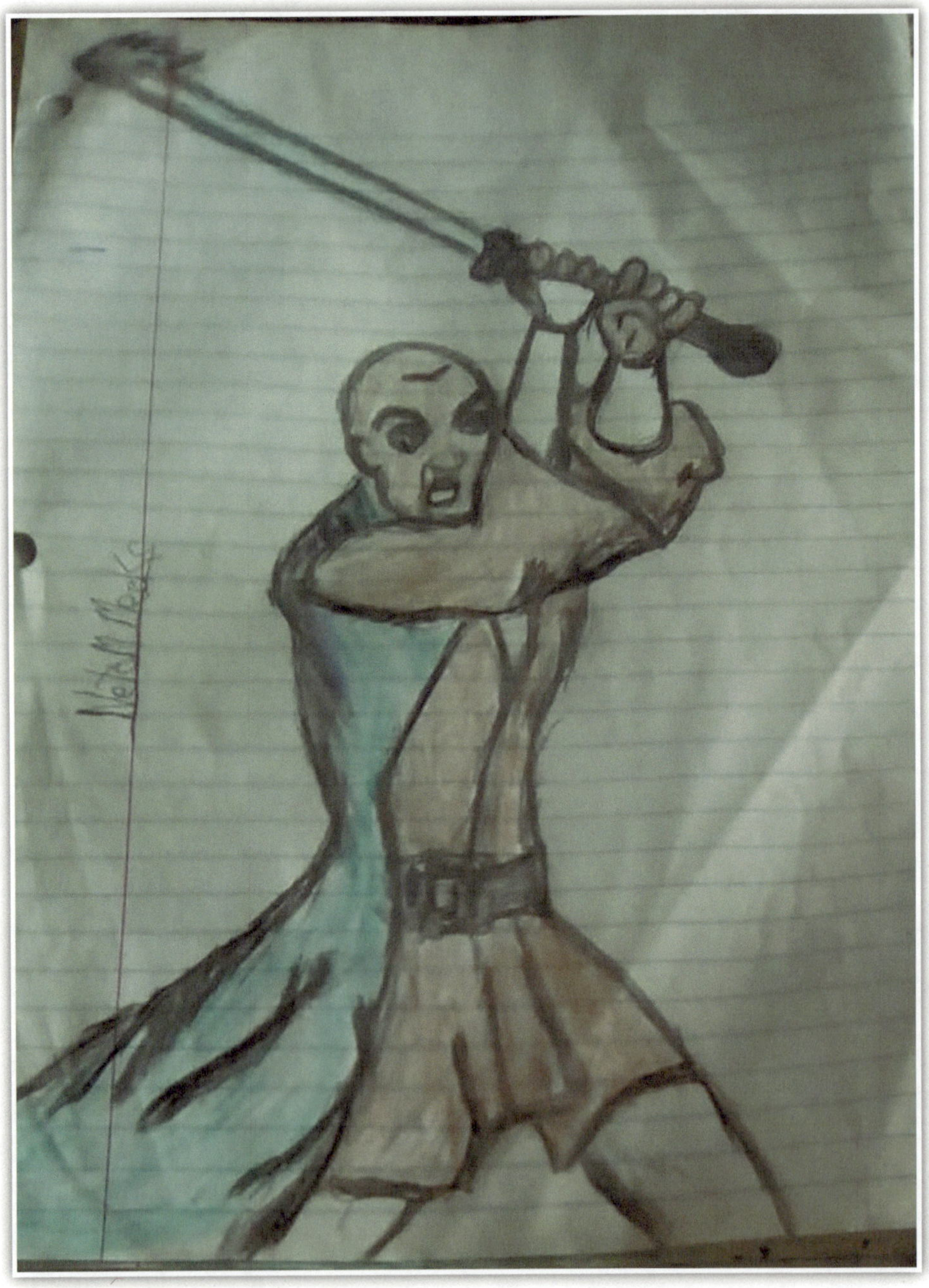

PART THREE

Hero

R.A.S.

Be Brave

Gotta be brave
Never be a slave
From the cradle to the grave
That's just my ways
Still the fire blaze
Hotter than a gauge
Mek way for the prophets of rage

Gotta be brave
Never be a slave
From the cradle to the grave
That's just my ways
Still the fire blaze
Hotter than a gauge
Mek way for the prophets of rage

Dem want I
Dem want I
Coulda dem funeral
Dem claim sey
Dem claim sey
Dem a de general
Rawyal AFRIIKAN SOULJAHS
Junior Reid - Indeed, Indeed, Indeed

Shango - you know, you know, you know
Garner Silk on a different level
Higher than the devil
Bring it back
Heart attack
Just like that
On a different level
Higher than the devil
Bring it back
Heart attack
Just like that

The music the music
Gotta play the music
The music the music
Don't abuse it
The music the music
Gotta play the music
The music the music
Don't abuse it

Dem want I
Coulda dem funeral
Dem claim say
Dem a general

I'm A Hero

I'm a hero if yu never know
Took a little time but now it's gotta show
I'm a hero
What's my name? Neto
No me nah go bow
Me sey me nah stoop low
I'm a hero
I'm a hero if yu never know
Took a little time but now it's gotta show
I'm a hero - What's my name? Neto
No meh nah go bow - meh seh
Meh nah stoop low - I'm a hero

Neto - like NEO when I enter the matrix
Me - I am the one son - no replacements
Me nah scared
Meh nah afraid of the CIA Agents
Dem higher than the sky
Dem lower than the basement
Peeps a ask Neto Meeks how the case went
Peeps a ask Neto Meeks if it was flagrant
Me focus, work hard and have patience
And align that now in the explanation

Chorus 2

I'm a hero- if ya never know

Took a little time but now it's gotta show

I'm a hero - What's my name? Neto

No me nah go bow - meh seh

Me nah stoop low - I'm a hero

You can ask Ibo

Can't stop the vibes from flow -yo

Mr Meeks, Mr Miracle, AKA Scott Free

Babylon do their best but they can't stop me

Serious as cancer,

Youths looking for the answer

So I guess I gotta be something like the Black Panther

I mean I'm an Avenger

And not a Pretender

You would meet Walter Rodney! Yo! I still remember

Self - defense

No pretense

So that means I'm a defender

But not the Ghost Rider more like

Coast to Coast Rider

No ghost represent

No boast just the toast but ya know I'm more liver than Spiderman

Hide the plan from the vultures,

Trying to steal the culture

So I'm like ultra

Madness in the Magnus

Burning out dem badness

I'm a hero, if ya never know
Took a little time but now it's gotta show
I'm a hero - what's my name Neto
No me nah go bow
Me seh me nah stoop low
I'm a hero

Dragon Fly

I heard this sound inside my house
It was not a roach a scorpion or a mouse
Beating against the window anxiously
The sounds of wings that desperately
wanted to fly free
Trapped by something you could not see
Wicked disguise
Invisible even to your many eyes
But was a barrier
Still
I turned on the light saw your plight
And in my fright thought kill, kill, kill, kill
What fearsome creature is this?
With wings that buzz and hiss
 And a tail that turn and twist
At the end I see a sting
Then
Faster than a stone
Thrown from the sling of an incient Warrior King
you flew
Not at me but towards the light
The light, the light, the light
The bulb above
If I had known love instead of fright

I would have understood your plight
And then everything would have been alright
Instead with a broom
I sealed your doom
Your life's final flight on the floor of my living room
Body smashed
I crushed your head to end your pain
But you, my armored friend
Head scattered on the floor
Drew breath
again
 again
 again
Your wings reflecting the light
Built so intricate beautiful delicate
reflecting the light red-gold-green
Maybe you saw my flag and entered the room
Because you figured we dig the same type of scene
I found out later
You're a mosquito-slayer, vampire-killer
Like the I
So I say a prayer
Forgive me Father
You may ask me why
Many a night
I've been bitten by a parasite
But never, never by a dragonfly

Field Marshall

R.A.S.
Some a dem is so jealous,
Overzealous,
Can't believe what they tell us,
Trying to take with these overpriced lies that they sell us.
Want Mi in the dust 'cause I'm Rebellious.
Another Day in Court,
To me it's my life, to them it's a sport,
But w hat's a Beauty Spot but A wart?
What is a thing but a thought...
Rome set dem internet lotta fish get caught.
My People sold and bought
But I learn more than I was taught or told,
Never sold my soul for the gold,
For my goals, I take control.
Following the code in my soul,
Across the Sea, we roll and paddle.
Ethiopian Palace,
Zimbabwe Castles,
Buffalo SoulJah in the saddle,
Black Cowboy lasso the cattle,
BoBo Shanti. Niyabinghi.
Man A Field; Marshal in the Battle....

Grow What You Eat!

Grow whe you eat and eat whe you grow
Seed whe you reap a de seed why u sow
If you never know well it's time that you know
It's me Neto Meeks with the new dub flow

From the seed to the plant from the plant to the plate
Not out of greed but out of need we have to strive to be great
Stay alive so we can make advancements for the people
Advancements for the race
Can't move without food, we want feed wi face
With food that's nutritious and delicious to the taste
Food deh ya nuff and we nuh want no food waste
We want it by the ton so we can pack it by the crate
Ship it overseas then send the g's back to mi place
Dinner time fine, alright say your grace
Give thanks and praise for the food on your plate
Give thanks and praise for the most high who create
The earth and the land the land and the soil
Gi wi corn fi plant, corn fi roast, corn fi boil
Corn fi sell and fatten up wi coil, due to ethonal
The price of corn worldwide going up all the while
Plant back the corn and feed the hungry child
To his face bring a smile

Royal African Soldier, now you should know my style
I learnt it from my ancestors on the banks of the Nile

Grow whe you eat and eat whe you grow
Seed whe you reap a de seed whey u sow
If you never know it's time that you know
It's me Neto Meeks with the new dub flow

A wha gwaan? It's like me can't keep calm
How everybody want eat but nobody want farm
Up the vineyard but dem want mow lawn?
Everything pretty but what a calamity
When yu can't find no food to eat in de city
Man a go nyam dog some done a nyam kitty
But we nuh gravalicious and we nuh licky licky
Bout anything whe we eat Rasta man very picky
Serious laughter don't want no food that's genetically altered
That's uncalled fah, them shoulda build a law fah
Here in this land of wood and water nobody musn't starve
Everybody get brawta
Teach the technique to your son and daughter
So they can prosper
Turn watch the money run come faster than Asafa

Grow whey u eat and eat whe yu grow
Seed whey u reap a de seat whey u sow
If yu never know it's time that yu know
It's me Neto Meeks with the new dub flow

Naturalness is natural bless
I need the natural herbs and fruits that's natural fresh
Our standards pass any actual test
From the east to the west, St Ann to St Bess
We want more food more farm more techno progress
I need a roof over my head and food on my table
After that we can get the DVD and the cable
We haffi keep it stable

Grow what yu eat and eat whey u sow
Seed whey u reap a di seed whey u sow
If yu never know it's time that yu know
It's me Neto Meeks with the new dub flow

Island, I Land

Jamaica, Jamaicans this land is ours
Full of magical moments and mystical powers
Lush green blessed by the steady rain showers
We're all brave hearts round here no cowards
That's how we made it across the seas and never
got devoured
By the great white sharks,
More time I reminisce about this looking at the stars
Shining through the dark, I know the past
Is what mek we step how we walk, talk how we chant
Enabling us to rise to the top of the charts
Jamaica, land of Marcus and Marley
The wise and de smart, the light and the dark
Blessed with the heart of a lion my people
Never will be torn apart
Jamaica land of wood and water, but right now
Our throats parched
And thirsty wondering if somebody curse we
Just a play, I know JAH bless JA, but where do the children play
When gunshot a stray all past de nursery?
So de ting set up. O.K., who plan it firstly?
Second question, how do we change it?
Answer; get the government to rearrange it
Yeah, represent cause our tax dollars make sense

Every man and woman in the land is the govament
The intent, make sure our representatives get the message sent
In the way that we meant, straight never bent
Redeem and repent, so I and I can rise from good to excellent, excellent, excellent.

Warriors

Calling all my warriors to the battlefield
Let me know if the blood inside your vein is real
Calling all my soldiers to the frontline
Hope you got your army and you're ready to shine
Calling all my warriors to the battlefield
Let me know if the blood inside your vein is real
Calling all my soldiers to the frontline
Hope you got your army and you're ready to shine
Calling all my warriors to the battlefield
Let me know if the blood inside your vein is real
Calling all my soldiers to the frontline
Hope you got your army and you're ready to shine

It's like a whole new beginning
That's Alpha
No Omega
We praise the Most High is fire pan de traitors
Rome try to break us
Still we remain courageous
Chop to the top like a one way elevator
Warrior, priests and kings
They know our status
Dis de programme anytime and try to under-rate us
It's your own loss

Yu die, pay the cost
Crucified on the cross
Among people who claim to be
Family
but was enemies
Yu wudden believe the culprits
who de cap fit
Even if dem standing on de pulpits
A oneness

Listen

Calling all my warriors to the battlefield
Let me know if the blood inside your vein is real
Calling all my soldiers to the frontline
Hope you got your army and you're ready to shine
Calling all my warriors to the battlefield
Let me know if the blood inside your vein is real
Calling all my soldiers to the frontline
Hope you got your army and you're ready to shine
Calling all my warriors to the battlefield
Let me know if the blood inside your vein is real
Calling all my soldiers to the frontline
Hope you got your army and you're ready to shine

See we
Running through pain
Never fraid of being enslaved
Making my escape
While lighting the fields aflame

Run to the hill
Not promised to make it

Still

In the Midnight Black
Blood on my back
A run naked
One chance to survive
No surprise if a take it
Like one sperm cell among millions
To the semen
Creation of life
My purpose
That I believe in
No time inna my mind
For the heathen
The powers to pulverize
The perpetrators who plan to weaken and
Infiltrate
Sudden death
The mind state
Oh Menen and Marcus Garvey I meditate
Keep it simple
Although they complicate
More time

Rate a get me irate
Very vex
Chains on our hands, feet and very necks

Delicate things destroyed

By dangerous delegates

The plan's intricate yet quite simple

My people sleeping longer than Rip Van Winkle

I'm shining like a diamond when I'm rhyming or a twinkle

Calling all my warriors to the battlefield

Let me know if the blood inside your vein is real

Calling all my soldiers to the frontline

Hope you got your army and you're ready to shine

Calling all my warriors to the battlefield

Let me know if the blood inside your vein is real

Calling all my soldiers to the frontline

Hope you got your army and you're ready to shine

Calling all my warriors to the battlefield

Let me know if the blood inside your vein is real

Calling all my soldiers to the frontline

Hope you got your army and you're ready to shine

It's like a whole new beginning

Alpha

No Omega

We praise the Most High

Blaze fire pan de traitors

Rome try to break us

Still we remain courageous

Top to top like one-way elevators

Warrior, priests and kings

They know our status

Dis de programme anytime and try to under rate us

It's your own loss
Yu die, pay the cost
Crucified on the cross
But we never take the loss
Calling all my warriors to the battlefield
Let me know if the blood inside your vein is real
Calling all my soldiers to the frontline
Hope you got your army and you're ready to shine
Calling all my warriors to the battlefield
Let me know if the blood inside your vein is real
Calling all my soldiers to the frontline

SO MUCH
THINGS
TO
SAY

Made in the USA
Columbia, SC
11 March 2025